# MAD LIBS®

## UPSIDE DOWN MAD LIBS

By Roger Price and Leonard Stern

W9-AYY-929

Mad Libs
An Imprint of Penguin Random House

MAD LIBS
Penguin Young Readers Group
An Imprint of Penguin Random House LLC

Concept created by Roger Price & Leonard Stern

Published by Mad Libs,
an imprint of Penguin Random House LLC,
345 Hudson Street, New York, New York 10014.
Printed in the USA.

ISBN 9780843139358
40

# MAD LIBS®
# INSTRUCTIONS

MAD LIBS® is a game for people who don't like games!
It can be played by one, two, three, four, or forty.

## • RIDICULOUSLY SIMPLE DIRECTIONS

In this tablet you will find stories containing blank spaces where words are left out. One player, the READER, selects one of these stories. The READER does not tell anyone what the story is about. Instead, he/she asks the other players, the WRITERS, to give him/her words. These words are used to fill in the blank spaces in the story.

## • TO PLAY

The READER asks each WRITER in turn to call out a word—an adjective or a noun or whatever the space calls for—and uses them to fill in the blank spaces in the story. The result is a MAD LIBS® game.

When the READER then reads the completed MAD LIBS® game to the other players, they will discover that they have written a story that is fantastic, screamingly funny, shocking, silly, crazy, or just plain dumb—depending upon which words each WRITER called out.

## • EXAMPLE (*Before* and *After*)

"_____ !" he said _____
　　　　EXCLAMATION　　　　　　　　　　　　　　　　ADVERB

as he jumped into his convertible _____ and
　　　　　　　　　　　　　　　　　　　　　　NOUN

drove off with his _____ wife.
　　　　　　　　　　ADJECTIVE

"_____*Ouch!*_____ !" he said _____*stupidly*_____
　　　　EXCLAMATION　　　　　　　　　　　　　　　ADVERB

as he jumped into his convertible _____*cat*_____ and
　　　　　　　　　　　　　　　　　　　　NOUN

drove off with his _____*brave*_____ wife.
　　　　　　　　　　ADJECTIVE

# MAD⊚LIBS®
# QUICK REVIEW

In case you have forgotten what adjectives, adverbs, nouns, and verbs are, here is a quick review:

An ADJECTIVE describes something or somebody. *Lumpy, soft, ugly, messy,* and *short* are adjectives.

An ADVERB tells how something is done. It modifies a verb and usually ends in "ly." *Modestly, stupidly, greedily,* and *carefully* are adverbs.

A NOUN is the name of a person, place or thing. *Sidewalk, umbrella, bridle, bathtub,* and *nose* are nouns.

A VERB is an action word. *Run, pitch, jump,* and *swim* are verbs. Put the verbs in past tense if the directions say PAST TENSE. *Ran, pitched, jumped,* and *swam* are verbs in the past tense.

When we ask for a PLACE, we mean any sort of place: a country or city *(Spain, Cleveland)* or a room *(bathroom, kitchen.)*

An EXCLAMATION or SILLY WORD is any sort of funny sound, gasp, grunt, or outcry, like *Wow!, Ouch!, Whomp!, Ick!,* and *Gadzooks!*

When we ask for specific words, like a NUMBER, a COLOR, an ANIMAL, or a PART OF THE BODY, we mean a word that is one of those things, like *seven, blue, horse,* or *head*.

When we ask for a PLURAL, it means more than one. For example, *cat* pluralized is *cats*.

MAD LIBS® is fun to play with friends, but you can also play it by yourself! To begin with, DO NOT look at the story on the page below. Fill in the blanks on this page with the words called for. Then, using the words you have selected, fill in the blank spaces in the story.

Now you've created your own hilarious MAD LIBS® game!

# RECIPE FOR
# AN UPSIDE-DOWN CAKE

ADJECTIVE _____

NOUN _____

NOUN _____

NUMBER _____

NOUN _____

ADJECTIVE _____

ADJECTIVE _____

ADJECTIVE _____

VERB _____

NOUN _____

ADVERB _____

PLURAL NOUN _____

NOUN _____

NOUN _____

VERB _____

NOUN _____

ADJECTIVE _____

VERB (PAST TENSE) _____

NOUN _____

# MAD LIBS®
# RECIPE FOR
# AN UPSIDE-DOWN CAKE

Here is a/an _____ recipe for an Upside-Down _____ .
<br>ADJECTIVE                                         NOUN

First, you preheat your _____ to _____ degrees. Then
<br>NOUN         NUMBER

take a stick of _____ and melt it in a ten-inch _____
<br>NOUN                          ADJECTIVE

skillet over a very _____ flame. In a/an _____ bowl
<br>ADJECTIVE                        ADJECTIVE

_____ granulated _____ and flour, stirring the mixture
<br>VERB                    NOUN

_____. Add milk and _____ and beat rapidly with
<br>ADVERB                PLURAL NOUN

an electric _____. Bake until your _____ is ready.
<br>NOUN                     NOUN

After the cake cools, _____ it from the _____
<br>VERB                       NOUN

and turn it upside-_____. Serve the cake warm with
<br>ADJECTIVE

_____ cream of small spoonfuls of _____ on top.
<br>VERB (PAST TENSE)                            NOUN

MAD LIBS® is fun to play with friends, but you can also play it by yourself! To begin with, DO NOT look at the story on the page below. Fill in the blanks on this page with the words called for. Then, using the words you have selected, fill in the blank spaces in the story.

Now you've created your own hilarious MAD LIBS® game!

# ALICE'S UPSIDE-DOWN WORLD

ADJECTIVE _____

NOUN _____

PLURAL NOUN _____

NUMBER _____

ADJECTIVE _____

VERB ENDING IN "S" _____

ADJECTIVE _____

NOUN _____

NOUN _____

NOUN _____

NOUN _____

VERB ENDING IN "S" _____

NOUN _____

ADJECTIVE _____

NOUN _____

PLURAL NOUN _____

ADJECTIVE _____

NOUN _____

# MAD LIBS®
# ALICE'S UPSIDE-DOWN WORLD

Lewis Carroll's classic, *Alice's Adventures in Wonderland*, as well as

its _____ sequel, *Through the Looking* _____,
    ADJECTIVE                               NOUN

have enchanted both the young and the old _____ for the
                                            PLURAL NOUN

last _____ years. Alice's _____ adventures begin when
      NUMBER              ADJECTIVE

she _____ down a/an _____ hole and lands
    VERB ENDING IN "S"                 ADJECTIVE

in a strange and topsy-turvy _____. There she discovers she
                           NOUN

can become a tall _____ or a small _____ simply by
              NOUN               NOUN

nibbling on alternate sides of a magic _____. In her travels
                               NOUN

through Wonderland, Alice _____ such remarkable
                    VERB ENDING IN "S"

characters as the White _____, the _____ Hatter,
                    NOUN          ADJECTIVE

the Cheshire _____, and even the Queen of _____.
            NOUN                     PLURAL NOUN

Unfortunately, Alice's adventures come to a/an _____ end
                                  ADJECTIVE

when Alice awakens from her _____.
                      NOUN

MAD LIBS® is fun to play with friends, but you can also play it by yourself! To begin with, DO NOT look at the story on the page below. Fill in the blanks on this page with the words called for. Then, using the words you have selected, fill in the blank spaces in the story.

Now you've created your own hilarious MAD LIBS® game!

# EAT, DRINK, AND BE SICK

NOUN _____

ADJECTIVE _____

ADJECTIVE _____

NOUN _____

NOUN _____

PLURAL NOUN _____

PLURAL NOUN _____

NOUN _____

PART OF THE BODY _____

PLURAL NOUN _____

ADVERB _____

PLURAL NOUN _____

PLURAL NOUN _____

PLURAL NOUN _____

LETTER OF THE ALPHABET _____

# MAD☺LIBS®
# EAT, DRINK, AND BE SICK

An inspector from the Department of Health and _____ Services
                                                NOUN

paid a surprise visit to our _____ school cafeteria. The lunch
                              ADJECTIVE

special, prepared by our _____ dietician, was spaghetti and
                          ADJECTIVE

_____-balls with a choice of either a/an _____ salad or
NOUN                                            NOUN

french _____. The inspector found the meat-_____
       PLURAL NOUN                                    PLURAL NOUN

to be overcooked and discovered a live _____ in the fries,
                                        NOUN

causing him to have a/an _____ ache. In response, he
                         PART OF THE BODY

threw up all over his _____. In his report, the inspector
                       PLURAL NOUN

_____ recommended that the school cafeteria serve only
ADVERB

nutritious _____ as well as low-calorie _____, and
           PLURAL NOUN                          PLURAL NOUN

that all of the saturated _____ be eliminated. He rated the
                          PLURAL NOUN

cafeteria a/an _____-minus.
               LETTER OF THE ALPHABET

MAD LIBS® is fun to play with friends, but you can also play it by yourself! To begin with, DO NOT look at the story on the page below. Fill in the blanks on this page with the words called for. Then, using the words you have selected, fill in the blank spaces in the story.

Now you've created your own hilarious MAD LIBS® game!

# THE OBSERVATORY

ADJECTIVE _____

NOUN _____

NOUN _____

NOUN _____

NOUN _____

PLURAL NOUN _____

PLURAL NOUN _____

VERB _____

PLURAL NOUN _____

PLURAL NOUN _____

NOUN _____

NOUN _____

ADJECTIVE _____

VERB _____

NOUN _____

# MAD☺LIBS®
# THE OBSERVATORY

Our class went on a field trip to a/an _____ observatory.
ADJECTIVE

It was located on top of a/an _____ , and it looked like a giant
NOUN

_____ with a slit down its _____ . We went inside
NOUN                                        NOUN

and looked through a/an _____ and were able to see
NOUN

_____ in the sky that were millions of _____
PLURAL NOUN                                            PLURAL NOUN

away. The men and women who _____ in the observa-
VERB

tory are called _____ , and they are always watching for
PLURAL NOUN

comets, eclipses, and shooting _____ . An eclipse occurs
PLURAL NOUN

when a/a _____ comes between the earth and the _____
NOUN                                                    NOUN

and everything gets _____ . Next week, we plan to
ADVERB

_____ the Museum of Modern _____ .
VERB                                    NOUN

MAD LIBS® is fun to play with friends, but you can also play it by yourself! To begin with, DO NOT look at the story on the page below. Fill in the blanks on this page with the words called for. Then, using the words you have selected, fill in the blank spaces in the story.

Now you've created your own hilarious MAD LIBS® game!

# UPSIDE-DOWN DICTIONARY STARTING WITH LETTER "A"

ADJECTIVE _____

PLURAL NOUN _____

ADJECTIVE _____

NOUN _____

NOUN _____

NOUN _____

ADJECTIVE _____

ADVERB _____

NOUN _____

PART OF THE BODY _____

ADJECTIVE _____

NOUN _____

NOUN _____

NOUN _____

*AARDVARK* (noun): A/An _____ mammal who feeds on ants
ADJECTIVE

and _____. The aardvark is squat and has a/an _____
PLURAL NOUN                                                                    ADJECTIVE

tongue and a long _____ ending in a round, piglike _____.
NOUN                                                                    NOUN

*ANGEL* (noun): A supernatural _____, either good or
NOUN

_____, who is _____ seen as a white-robed
ADJECTIVE                                  ADVERB

_____ with wings over his or her _____.
NOUN                                                            PART OF THE BODY

*ASTRONAUT* (noun): Sometimes a/an _____ scientist, but
ADJECTIVE

usually an army or navy _____ trained to make flights to
NOUN

the _____ in a space _____.
NOUN                              NOUN

MAD LIBS® is fun to play with friends, but you can also play it by yourself! To begin with, DO NOT look at the story on the page below. Fill in the blanks on this page with the words called for. Then, using the words you have selected, fill in the blank spaces in the story.

Now you've created your own hilarious MAD LIBS® game!

# CAR OF THE YEAR

PERSON IN ROOM (LAST NAME) _____

NOUN _____

NOUN _____

PLURAL NOUN _____

PLURAL NOUN _____

PLURAL NOUN _____

PLURAL NOUN _____

TYPE OF LIQUID _____

NOUN _____

VERB _____

SAME LAST NAME _____

PART OF THE BODY (PLURAL) _____

NOUN _____

ADJECTIVE_____

NOUN _____

EXCLAMATION_____

# MAD☉LIBS®
# CAR OF THE YEAR

It's here, the all-new _____. The most luxurious
PERSON IN ROOM (LAST NAME)

_____ you'll ever drive! The only four-door _____ that
NOUN                                                    NOUN

comes equipped with dual air _____, power _____,
PLURAL NOUN                          PLURAL NOUN

and contoured, plush leather _____. And, believe it or not,
PLURAL NOUN

it is the only car in its class that can go up to a hundred thousand

_____ without needing a/an _____ change or
PLURAL NOUN                             TYPE OF LIQUID

a/an _____ tune-up. Run, do not _____ to your nearest
NOUN                                          VERB

_____ dealer and feast your _____ on
SAME LAST NAME                              PART OF THE BODY (PLURAL)

the car that *Motor* _____ magazine calls the _____
NOUN                                        ADJECTIVE

_____ of the year. As always, we save the best for last: When
NOUN

you see the sticker price, you are sure to shout, "_____!"
EXCLAMATION

MAD LIBS® is fun to play with friends, but you can also play it by yourself! To begin with, DO NOT look at the story on the page below. Fill in the blanks on this page with the words called for. Then, using the words you have selected, fill in the blank spaces in the story.

Now you've created your own hilarious MAD LIBS® game!

# GREAT EXCUSES FOR BEING LATE

ADJECTIVE _____

PERSON IN ROOM _____

VERB ENDING IN "ING" _____

PART OF THE BODY _____

NOUN _____

NOUN _____

NUMBER _____

PLURAL NOUN _____

TYPE OF LIQUID _____

ADVERB _____

ANOTHER PERSON IN ROOM _____

ADJECTIVE _____

ADJECTIVE _____

SAME PERSON IN ROOM _____

ADJECTIVE _____

ADJECTIVE _____

ADJECTIVE _____

PLURAL NOUN _____

NOUN _____

PLURAL NOUN _____

VERB _____

PLURAL NOUN _____

# MAD LIBS®
# GREAT EXCUSES
# FOR BEING LATE

Dear Physical Education Teacher,

Please excuse my son/daughter from missing _____ class
ADJECTIVE

yesterday. When _____ awakened yesterday, I could
PERSON IN ROOM

see that his/her nose was _____. He/She also complained
ADJECTIVE

of _____ aches and having a sore _____, and I took
PART OF THE BODY                                          NOUN

him/her to the family _____. The doctor quickly diagnosed
NOUN

it to be the _____-hour flu and suggested he/her take two
NUMBER

_____ with a glass of _____ and go to bed _____.
PLURAL NOUN                        TYPE OF LIQUID                            ADVERB


Dear Science Teacher,

Please excuse _____ for being late for your
ANOTHER PERSON IN ROOM

_____ science class. It's my fault. I feel _____.
ADJECTIVE                                                        ADJECTIVE

_____ was up until the _____ hours of the
SAME PERSON IN ROOM                              ADJECTIVE

morning completing his/her _____ project. Just as he/she was
ADJECTIVE

going out the _____ door, I noticed that his/her only pair of
ADJECTIVE

_____ had a/an _____ in them. It took me an hour to
PLURAL NOUN                        NOUN

find my _____ so I could see to _____ the needle,
PLURAL NOUN                                                  VERB

enabling me to sew his/her _____ back together.
PLURAL NOUN

MAD LIBS® is fun to play with friends, but you can also play it by yourself! To begin with, DO NOT look at the story on the page below. Fill in the blanks on this page with the words called for. Then, using the words you have selected, fill in the blank spaces in the story.

Now you've created your own hilarious MAD LIBS® game!

## SPEAKING OF SPEAKING

ADJECTIVE _____

VERB ENDING IN "ING" _____

PLURAL NOUN _____

NOUN _____

PLURAL NOUN _____

ADJECTIVE _____

PLURAL NOUN _____

PLURAL NOUN _____

NOUN _____

NOUN _____

PART OF THE BODY _____

ADJECTIVE _____

ADJECTIVE _____

PART OF THE BODY _____

TYPE OF LIQUID _____

PART OF THE BODY _____

# MAD☺LIBS®
# SPEAKING OF SPEAKING

A recent _____ poll shows that the majority of people are
          ADJECTIVE

terrified of public _____. They would rather walk
                    VERB ENDING IN "ING"

across burning _____ or swim in _____-infested
               PLURAL NOUN                NOUN

waters than give a speech in front of a group of _____. This
                                                 PLURAL NOUN

_____ fear can be overcome in five easy _____:
 ADJECTIVE                                        PLURAL NOUN

1. Organize all of your _____ on a piece of _____.
                        PLURAL NOUN                   NOUN

2. Remember to start your speech with a funny _____.
                                              NOUN

3. When speaking, look your audience straight in the _____
                                                     PART OF THE BODY

   and speak in a strong and _____ voice.
                             ADJECTIVE

4. Be simple. Never use _____ words that are over the
                        ADJECTIVE

   audience's _____.
              PART OF THE BODY

5. Always keep a pitcher of _____ next to you, in case your
                            TYPE OF LIQUID

   _____ goes dry.
   PART OF THE BODY

MAD LIBS® is fun to play with friends, but you can also play it by yourself! To begin with, DO NOT look at the story on the page below. Fill in the blanks on this page with the words called for. Then, using the words you have selected, fill in the blank spaces in the story.

Now you've created your own hilarious MAD LIBS® game!

# VIDEO GAMES

VERB _____

NOUN _____

NOUN _____

VERB ENDING IN "ING" _____

NOUN _____

ADJECTIVE_____

PART OF THE BODY _____

PLURAL NOUN _____

ADJECTIVE_____

PART OF THE BODY _____

PLURAL NOUN _____

ADJECTIVE_____

PLURAL NOUN _____

ADJECTIVE_____

NUMBER _____

NOUN _____

PLURAL NOUN _____

# MAD LIBS®
# VIDEO GAMES

I love to _____ video games. I can play them day and
_____VERB_____

_____! My mom and _____ are not too happy with my
NOUN                              NOUN

_____ so much time in front of the television _____.
VERB ENDING IN "ING"                                                      NOUN

Although Dad believes that these _____ games help children
                                         ADJECTIVE

develop hand-_____ coordination and improve their
                  PART OF THE BODY

learning _____, he also seems to think they have _____
           PLURAL NOUN                                          ADJECTIVE

side effects on one's _____. Both of my _____
                        PART OF THE BODY                        PLURAL NOUN

think this is due to a/an _____ use of violence in the majority
                            ADJECTIVE

of the _____. Finally, we all arrived at a/an _____
          PLURAL NOUN                                          ADJECTIVE

compromise: After dinner I can play _____ hours of video games,
                                        NUMBER

provided I help clear the _____ and wash the _____.
                            NOUN                         PLURAL NOUN

MAD LIBS® is fun to play with friends, but you can also play it by yourself! To begin with, DO NOT look at the story on the page below. Fill in the blanks on this page with the words called for. Then, using the words you have selected, fill in the blank spaces in the story.

Now you've created your own hilarious MAD LIBS® game!

# AN ART NAMED MARTIAL

PLURAL NOUN _____

ADJECTIVE_____

PERSON IN ROOM _____

ADJECTIVE_____

NOUN _____

ADJECTIVE_____

PLURAL NOUN _____

ANIMAL _____

VERB _____

NOUN _____

NOUN _____

PART OF THE BODY_____

NOUN _____

NOUN _____

PART OF THE BODY (PLURAL) _____

# MAD LIBS®
# AN ART NAMED MARTIAL

Want to become an expert in Karate or Kung Fu?  You can learn

martial _____ in three _____ lessons with Master
       PLURAL NOUN             ADJECTIVE

_____ 's video tape. This _____-selling tape
  PERSON IN ROOM                     ADJECTIVE

takes you step-by-_____ through a series of _____
                 NOUN                      ADJECTIVE

exercises guaranteed to develop _____ in your body and
                                PLURAL NOUN

make you strong as a/an _____.  In less than a week, you will
                      ANIMAL

be able to do one hundred _____-ups a day, skip a jumping
                          VERB

_____ for an hour, and climb a _____ without losing your
 NOUN                          NOUN

_____.  And believe it or not, by the end of the month,
 PART OF THE BODY

you'll not only be eligible for a black _____, but be capable
                              NOUN

of breaking a four-inch-thick _____ easily with your own
                           NOUN

two _____!
    PART OF THE BODY (PLURAL)

MAD LIBS® is fun to play with friends, but you can also play it by yourself! To begin with, DO NOT look at the story on the page below. Fill in the blanks on this page with the words called for. Then, using the words you have selected, fill in the blank spaces in the story.

Now you've created your own hilarious MAD LIBS® game!

# THE FARM

ADJECTIVE _____

NOUN _____

PLURAL NOUN _____

VERB _____

NOUN _____

ADJECTIVE _____

PLURAL NOUN _____

VERB _____

PLURAL NOUN _____

NOUN _____

NOUN _____

VERB _____

# MAD LIBS®
# THE FARM

I spent last summer on my grandfather's _____ farm. He
                                             ADJECTIVE

raises oats, wheat, and _____ . Grandfather also grows lettuce,
                              NOUN

corn, and lima _____ . My favorite place to _____ on
                   PLURAL NOUN                                VERB

the farm is the _____ house where Grandfather keeps his
                      NOUN

_____ chickens. Every day, each hen lays round, smooth
      ADJECTIVE

_____ . Grandfather sells most of them, but keeps some so
   PLURAL NOUN

the hens can _____ on them and hatch cute, fuzzy little
                    VERB

_____ . I'm looking forward to next year, when Grandfather
   PLURAL NOUN

is going to show me how to drive his _____ , sow the
                                            NOUN

_____ , and _____ the cow.
    NOUN                  VERB

MAD LIBS® is fun to play with friends, but you can also play it by yourself! To begin with, DO NOT look at the story on the page below. Fill in the blanks on this page with the words called for. Then, using the words you have selected, fill in the blank spaces in the story.

Now you've created your own hilarious MAD LIBS® game!

# VCR REMOTE CONTROL, WHERE ART THOU?

PLURAL NOUN _____

NOUN _____

NOUN _____

NOUN _____

PLURAL NOUN _____

PLURAL NOUN _____

PART OF BODY (PLURAL) _____

NOUN _____

NOUN _____

NOUN _____

VERB (PAST TENSE)_____

NOUN _____

ADJECTIVE_____

ADJECTIVE_____

# MAD☻LIBS®
# VCR REMOTE CONTROL, WHERE ART THOU?

A recent nationwide survey of over one hundred thousand _____
<br>PLURAL NOUN

shows that the three articles most often misplaced are a woman's

hand _____ , keys to the _____ , and most of all, the
<br>NOUN                  NOUN

videocassette recorder _____ . The first place to look for your
<br>NOUN

missing remote is the couch. Check behind the _____ , in be-
<br>PLURAL NOUN

tween the _____ , and if necessary, get down on your hands
<br>PLURAL NOUN

and _____ and look under the _____ or coffee
<br>PART OF THE BODY (PLURAL)                NOUN

_____ . Believe it or not, remotes have been found in such odd
<br>NOUN

places as the inside of a/an _____ , _____ under a
<br>NOUN             VERB (PAST TENSE)

pile of magazines, or floating in the bathroom _____ . If you
<br>NOUN

can't find your _____ remote, don't feel too bad...at least you
<br>ADJECTIVE

don't have to try to figure out how the _____ thing works!
<br>ADJECTIVE

MAD LIBS® is fun to play with friends, but you can also play it by yourself! To begin with, DO NOT look at the story on the page below. Fill in the blanks on this page with the words called for. Then, using the words you have selected, fill in the blank spaces in the story.

Now you've created your own hilarious MAD LIBS® game!

---

# SHOW AND TELL

NOUN _____

VERB ENDING IN "ING" _____

ADVERB _____

SOMETHING ALIVE _____

NOUN _____

ADJECTIVE _____

VERB _____

PERSON IN ROOM _____

ADJECTIVE _____

NOUN _____

SOMETHING TO EAT _____

VERB ENDING IN "ING" _____

PLURAL NOUN_____

NOUN _____

NUMBER_____

# MAD LIBS®
# SHOW AND TELL

Today, I would like to show the class a/an _____ I caught when
<u>NOUN</u>

I went _____ with my aunt. I had never fished before,
<u>VERB ENDING IN "ING"</u>

but my aunt _____ taught me how to bait a hook with a/an
<u>ADVERB</u>

_____ and then how to cast the _____ into the
<u>SOMETHING ALIVE</u>                                      <u>NOUN</u>

_____ lake. I _____ fishing!
<u>ADJECTIVE</u>              <u>VERB</u>


My name is _____, and I would like to show the
<u>PERSON IN ROOM</u>

class this _____ _____ from my mother's kitchen.
<u>ADJECTIVE</u>        <u>NOUN</u>

My mother uses it every morning to fix my _____. It is
<u>SOMETHING TO EAT</u>

also useful if you are into _____ or if you want to slice
<u>VERB ENDING IN "ING"</u>

up some _____. If you want one, you can buy it at your
<u>PLURAL NOUN</u>

local _____ store for only _____ dollars.
<u>NOUN</u>                          <u>NUMBER</u>

MAD LIBS® is fun to play with friends, but you can also play it by yourself! To begin with, DO NOT look at the story on the page below. Fill in the blanks on this page with the words called for. Then, using the words you have selected, fill in the blank spaces in the story.

Now you've created your own hilarious MAD LIBS® game!

# GOOD TO THE LAST BYTE

ANIMAL _____

ADJECTIVE_____

ADJECTIVE_____

NOUN _____

PLURAL NOUN _____

VERB _____

PLURAL NOUN _____

VERB _____

ADJECTIVE_____

PART OF THE BODY _____

PART OF THE BODY _____

NOUN _____

NOUN _____

# MAD LIBS®
# GOOD TO THE LAST BYTE

To be able to use a computer, you must have a keyboard, a monitor,

and a hand-held tracking device called a/an _____ . In
                                          ANIMAL

order to operate your _____ computer, a/an _____
                       ADJECTIVE                     ADJECTIVE

disk or a floppy _____ are essential.  Computers are very
                  NOUN

helpful for students because they store a million _____
                                                   PLURAL NOUN

of information in their hard _____ and correct misspelled
                             VERB

_____ . They can also add, subtract, and _____ numbers.
PLURAL NOUN                                        VERB

Now, computers come in every shape and size, big and _____ .
                                                      ADJECTIVE

The laptop computer, which sits on your _____ , is small
                                         PART OF THE BODY

enough that you can tuck it under your _____ or carry
                                        PART OF THE BODY

it to school in your _____ bag. Today, the computer is as much
                      NOUN

a part of a household as the kitchen _____ .
                                      NOUN

MAD LIBS® is fun to play with friends, but you can also play it by yourself! To begin with, DO NOT look at the story on the page below. Fill in the blanks on this page with the words called for. Then, using the words you have selected, fill in the blank spaces in the story.

Now you've created your own hilarious MAD LIBS® game!

# UPSIDE-DOWN DICTIONARY STARTING WITH LETTER "B"

ADJECTIVE _____

NOUN _____

NOUN _____

NOUN _____

ADJECTIVE _____

PLURAL NOUN _____

ADVERB _____

NOUN _____

VERB (PAST TENSE) _____

NOUN _____

PLURAL NOUN _____

ADVERB _____

NOUN _____

# MAD LIBS®
# UPSIDE-DOWN DICTIONARY
# STARTING WITH LETTER "B"

*BALLOON* (noun): A/An _____ bag that rises in the
ADJECTIVE

_____ when it is filled with hot _____.
NOUN                                                   NOUN

*BAGEL* (noun): A glazed _____-shaped roll with a/an
NOUN

_____ texture, made from _____ that are dropped
ADJECTIVE                                      PLURAL NOUN

into _____ boiling _____ and then baked.
ADVERB                          NOUN

*BASEBALL* (noun): A game _____ with a bat and a/an
VERB (PAST TENSE)

_____ by two teams of nine _____ each. These
NOUN                                              PLURAL NOUN

two teams play _____ in the _____ and at bat.
ADVERB                          NOUN

MAD LIBS® is fun to play with friends, but you can also play it by yourself! To begin with, DO NOT look at the story on the page below. Fill in the blanks on this page with the words called for. Then, using the words you have selected, fill in the blank spaces in the story.

Now you've created your own hilarious MAD LIBS® game!

# THE PROM

PART OF THE BODY _____

PART OF THE BODY _____

ADJECTIVE _____

ADJECTIVE _____

NOUN _____

NOUN _____

VERB (PAST TENSE) _____

PLURAL NOUN _____

NOUN _____

NOUN _____

PLURAL NOUN _____

ADJECTIVE _____

VERB ENDING IN "ING" _____

ADJECTIVE _____

NOUN _____

NOUN _____

NOUN _____

# MAD LIBS®
# THE PROM

If there's a melody you can't seem to get out of your _____
PART OF THE BODY

or a song running through your _____, then bring your
PART OF THE BODY

feet to this year's _____ prom. As usual, our _____
ADJECTIVE                                    NOUN

will be held in our high school _____. A dress code will be
NOUN

observed. No one will be admitted wearing _____ or
VERB (PAST TENSE)

torn _____. Girls must wear a/an _____ and
PLURAL NOUN                              NOUN

boys must wear a dress shirt and a/an _____. As always, hot
NOUN

_____ will be served, and there will be _____
PLURAL NOUN                                            ADJECTIVE

prizes and an award for the best-_____ couple. The
VERB ENDING IN "ING"

_____ dance committee is also proud to announce that
ADJECTIVE

every girl who attends will receive a/an _____ to pin to her
NOUN

_____, and every boy will receive a complimentary _____.
NOUN                                                        NOUN

MAD LIBS® is fun to play with friends, but you can also play it by yourself! To begin with, DO NOT look at the story on the page below. Fill in the blanks on this page with the words called for. Then, using the words you have selected, fill in the blank spaces in the story.

Now you've created your own hilarious MAD LIBS® game!

# TO WHOM IT MAY CONCERN

PERSON IN ROOM _____

NUMBER _____

ADVERB_____

NOUN _____

ADJECTIVE_____

VERB _____

ADJECTIVE_____

PLURAL NOUN _____

SAME PERSON IN ROOM_____

NOUN _____

PLURAL NOUN _____

NUMBER _____

SAME PERSON IN ROOM_____

ADJECTIVE_____

NOUN _____

VERB _____

# MAD LIBS®
# TO WHOM IT MAY CONCERN

I have known _____ for _____ years and _____
       PERSON IN ROOM      NUMBER         ADVERB

recommend him/her for the position of assistant _____ in your
                                              NOUN

_____ company. I can't _____ enough about this person's
ADJECTIVE                VERB

_____ character and ability to get along with his/her fellow
ADJECTIVE

_____. As for educational background, _____
PLURAL NOUN                           SAME PERSON IN ROOM

is a college _____, is capable of speaking several foreign
              NOUN

_____, and has an IQ of _____. You will find
PLURAL NOUN                     NUMBER

_____ to be a/an _____ worker who is not only
SAME PERSON IN ROOM         ADJECTIVE

as smart as a/an _____, but who doesn't know the meaning of
           NOUN

the word _____. Unfortunately, this is one of many words
       VERB

this person doesn't know the meaning of.

MAD LIBS® is fun to play with friends, but you can also play it by yourself! To begin with, DO NOT look at the story on the page below. Fill in the blanks on this page with the words called for. Then, using the words you have selected, fill in the blank spaces in the story.

Now you've created your own hilarious MAD LIBS® game!

# COMPUTERSPEAK

NOUN _____

PLURAL NOUN _____

VERB _____

NOUN _____

WORD BEGINNING WITH "M" _____

PLURAL NOUN _____

PLURAL NOUN _____

NOUN _____

VERB _____

PLURAL NOUN _____

NOUN _____

ADVERB_____

NOUN _____

ADJECTIVE_____

PLURAL NOUN _____

NOUN _____

# MAD LIBS®
# COMPUTERSPEAK

If you want to become _____ literate, here are some key
<br>NOUN

_____ that you should _____ as quickly as possible:
<br>PLURAL NOUN — VERB

*CD ROM*: Stands for compact _____ ... read only
<br>NOUN

_____ . This compact disc can hold as many as 600
<br>WORD BEGINNING WITH "M"

_____ , which is the equivalent of 700 floppy _____ .
<br>PLURAL NOUN — PLURAL NOUN

*CYBERSPACE*: Stands for the imaginary _____ that people
<br>NOUN

enter when they _____ with each other through computers on
<br>VERB

a collection of _____ , known as the Inter _____ .
<br>PLURAL NOUN — NOUN

*E-MAIL*: Means _____ transmitted _____ .
<br>ADVERB — NOUN

*MODEM*: Is the device that allows a/an _____ computer to
<br>ADJECTIVE

transmit _____ over a phone _____ .
<br>PLURAL NOUN — NOUN

MAD LIBS® is fun to play with friends, but you can also play it by yourself! To begin with, DO NOT look at the story on the page below. Fill in the blanks on this page with the words called for. Then, using the words you have selected, fill in the blank spaces in the story.

Now you've created your own hilarious MAD LIBS® game!

# MORE GREAT EXCUSES FOR TARDINESS

ADJECTIVE_____

PERSON IN ROOM (FIRST NAME)_____

ADJECTIVE_____

ANIMAL _____

ADJECTIVE_____

NUMBER _____

PART OF THE BODY (PLURAL) _____

ANOTHER PERSON (FIRST NAME) _____

PLURAL NOUN _____

NOUN _____

NOUN _____

ADJECTIVE_____

VERB (PAST TENSE)_____

NOUN _____

NOUN _____

ADJECTIVE_____

# MAD☺LIBS®
# MORE GREAT EXCUSES
# FOR TARDINESS

Dear Principal,

I am sorry to have to tell you that my _____ son/daughter,
<u>ADJECTIVE</u>

_____ will be unable to attend your _____
<u>PERSON IN ROOM (FIRST NAME)</u>                                    <u>ADJECTIVE</u>

school this week as he/she has caught a case of the _____ pox.
<u>ANIMAL</u>

The _____ doctor says that it will be _____ weeks before
<u>ADJECTIVE</u>                              <u>NUMBER</u>

he/she is healthy and back on his/her _____ again.
<u>PART OF THE BODY (PLURAL)</u>


Dear Math Teacher,

I was driving _____ to school when the
<u>ANOTHER PERSON (FIRST NAME)</u>

_____ failed and my car crashed into a/an _____. By
<u>PLURAL NOUN</u>                                    <u>NOUN</u>

the time the tow _____ finally arrived and the _____
<u>NOUN</u>                                    <u>ADJECTIVE</u>

mechanic _____ the _____ and recharged the
<u>VERB (PAST TENSE)</u>              <u>NOUN</u>

_____ , we had missed your _____ class.
<u>NOUN</u>                              <u>ADJECTIVE</u>

MAD LIBS® is fun to play with friends, but you can also play it by yourself! To begin with, DO NOT look at the story on the page below. Fill in the blanks on this page with the words called for. Then, using the words you have selected, fill in the blank spaces in the story.

Now you've created your own hilarious MAD LIBS® game!

# BICYCLE RIDING

VERB ENDING IN "ING" _____

ADJECTIVE _____

PLURAL NOUN _____

PART OF THE BODY _____

ADVERB _____

PART OF THE BODY _____

ADJECTIVE _____

NOUN _____

PLURAL NOUN _____

VERB _____

PLURAL NOUN _____

NOUN _____

NOUN _____

PART OF THE BODY _____

VERB _____

# MAD LIBS®
# BICYCLE RIDING

Most doctors agree that bicycle _____ is a/an
                                 VERB ENDING IN "ING"

_____ form of exercise that benefits _____ of all ages.
ADJECTIVE                                  PLURAL NOUN

Riding a bicycle enables you to develop your _____ mus-
                                              PART OF THE BODY

cles as well as _____ increase the rate of your _____
                 ADVERB                              PART OF THE BODY

beat.  Bicycle riding as also a/an _____ means of _____.
                                    ADJECTIVE                NOUN

More _____ around the world _____ bicycles than
      PLURAL NOUN                     VERB

drive _____.  No matter what kind of _____ you ride,
       PLURAL NOUN                             NOUN

always be sure to wear a/an _____ on your head and have re-
                             NOUN

flectors on your _____, especially if you _____ at night.
                  PART OF THE BODY                  VERB

# Join the millions of Mad Libs fans creating wacky and wonderful stories on our apps!

# Download Mad Libs today!